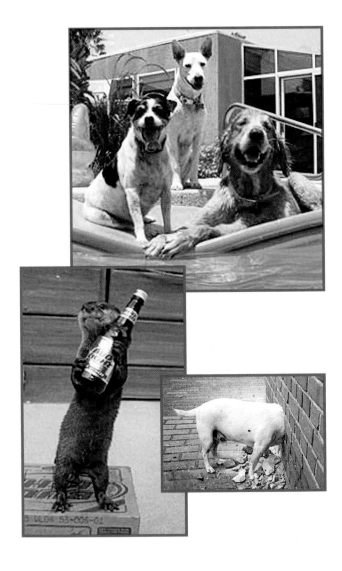

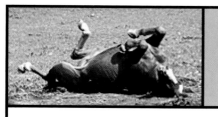

WHAT PETS DO WHILE YOU'RE AT WORK

**Jason Bergund
and Bev West**

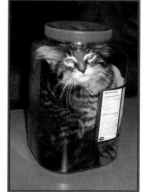

SCRIBNER

New York   London   Toronto   Sydney

SCRIBNER
A Division of Simon & Schuster, Inc.
1230 Avenue of the Americas
New York, NY 10020

First Scribner paperback edition October 2007

SCRIBNER and design are trademarks of
Macmillan Library Reference USA, Inc., used under license
by Simon & Schuster, the publisher of this work.

For information about special discounts for bulk purchases,
please contact Simon & Schuster Special Sales:
1-800-456-6798 or business@simonandschuster.com.

Manufactured in the United States of America

1   3   5   7   9   10   8   6   4   2

Library of Congress Control Number: 2007014587

ISBN-13: 978-1-4165-4756-3
ISBN-10: 1-4165-4756-8

Acknowledgments

Bev and Jason would like to thank our incomparable editor, Beth Wareham, for her insight, encouragement, and wicked sense of humor. Beth, we feel so lucky to have you. We would also like to give a shout-out to Kate Bittman for her enthusiasm and energy, to John Fulbrook and Erich Hobbing for their unerring design sense, and to Kim Doi for always having our backs. Thanks also to all of the pet parents and pets who have lent their pictures and stories to this book. Finally, a very special thanks to Jenny Bent, who once again gets our vote for the Best Agent in the World award.

To our pets,
Daisy, Elvis, Bert, Buddha, and Hamlet,
who remind us every day how to live each moment
to the fullest, especially when no one's looking.

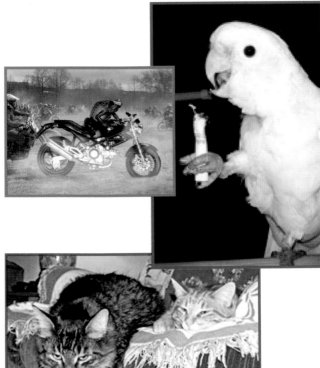
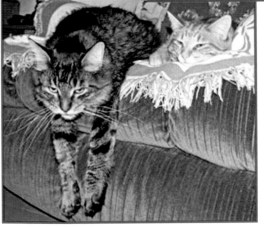

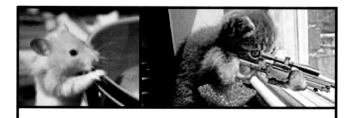

WHAT PETS DO WHILE YOU'RE AT WORK

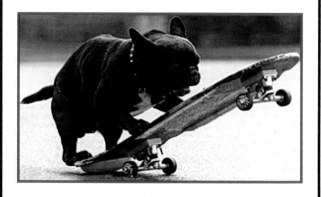

Introduction

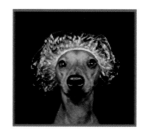

We know. It's terrible going off to work every morning and leaving your pets home alone. You carry the memory of those puppy-dog eyes or those sad kitty faces all the way to the office. You imagine them, waiting patiently and miserably by the door, anticipating the sound of your footfall on the stair, longing to leap up and greet you joyfully when you finally return from the trenches.

Boy, have they got you fooled!

In our unauthorized album of caught-in-the-act photos that pets never meant for us to see, you'll discover that our faithful companions are not languishing in the doorway desperately awaiting our return, as they would like us to believe. Pets are finding all sorts of ways to entertain themselves, and it isn't all good clean fun.

From bulldogs on the bottle to card-hustling kitties and Web-surfing huskies, the pets in these pages really don't seem to be missing us much at all. You can feel a little less guilty tomorrow morning when you head off to the salt mines, because chances are that your pets will be at home having themselves one hell of a good time and not giving you a second thought.

After all, when the masters are away . . . the pets will play.

While Dave is off assembling carburetors, Busta breaks it down.

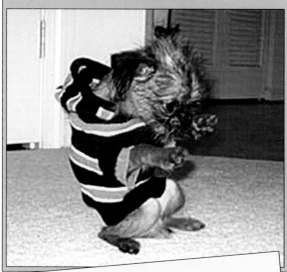

Name: Busta Move

Homepound: New Yorkie

Career Objective: Lil Romeo of the canine crowd

Current Occupation: Daddy's smushy-faced puppykins

Pet Parent: Dave S., mechanic

Fed up with Donna's long hours at a well-known women's fashion magazine, Betty gets ugly.

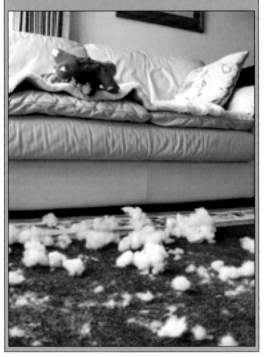

UPON HEARING THAT AMANDA HAS TO WORK LATE AGAIN, HONEYDEW COPS A 'TUDE.

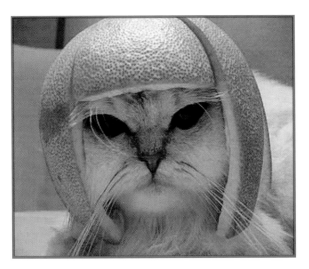

Whenever Sharon works a double, Chanterelle helps herself to a rejuvenating mask. Okay, so it's $200 an ounce and imported, but crested hairless dogs have to be fastidious about their complexions. And besides, she's worth it.

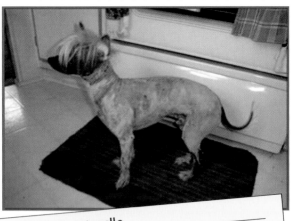

Name: Chanterelle

Favorite Movie: Gentlemen Prefer Blondes

Career Objective: High-maintenance bitch

Signature Champagne: Dog Perignon

Pet Parent: Sharon L., hair stylist

WHILE ANGIE IS ARGUING FOR THE DEFENSE, PIPER TAKES A LOOK AT THINGS FROM BOTH SIDES NOW.

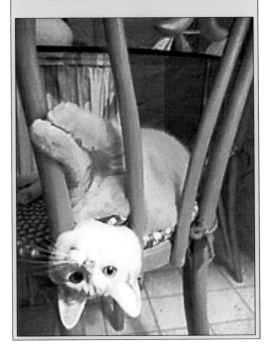

RAD LOOKS
FOR THE BIG AIR.

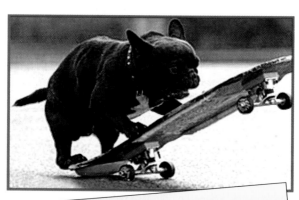

Name: Rad

AKA: Crazy Bastard

Homepound: Torrance, California

Personal Mantra: Hang 20

Pet Parent: Spike, airline reservations agent

**If you're wondering
what these bunnies are doing
while Stan's at work,**

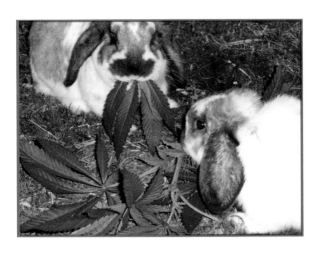

go ask Alice.

In a moment never before caught on tape, Sylvester demonstrates his invincible flying tiger kick.

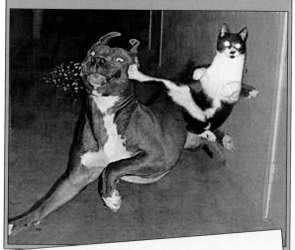

Name: Sylvester

AKA: Rambo

Homepound: Wherever you least expect him

Special Skill: Black belt in Cat Kwan Do

Pet Parents: Jim and JoAnne, customer service reps

No matter how hectic her schedule becomes, Stella always finds time to touch up her roots.

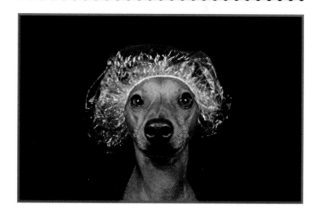

When Bernice
forgets her desktop Jesus
on Office Bible Study Day,
Annabelle discovers she really loves
Jesus too, even though he makes
her tongue tickle.

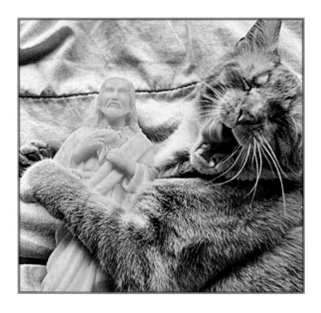

WHILE KARL'S BUSY
IN THE SITUATION ROOM,
RONNIE AND NANCY
ACT UP.

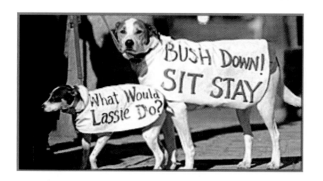

Now that Lorraine has closed the deal
on the Pine Street McMansion,
Boots prays for a better doghouse.

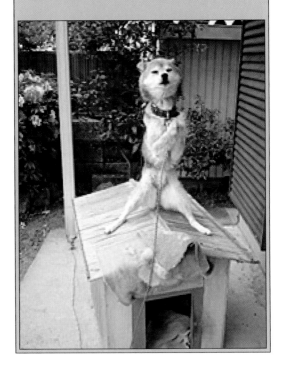

**Noid works on his Andy Warhol
impression.**

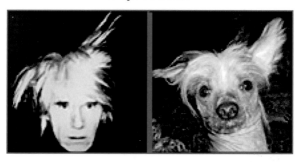

**He does Carol Channing too,
but only when no one is looking.**

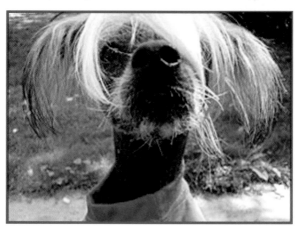

Minou discovers what Chef Antoine has really been putting in her Tuna Surprise.

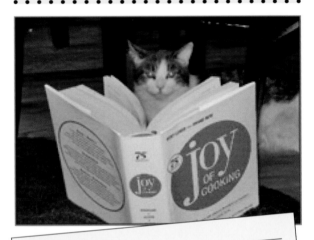

Name: Minou

AKA: Finicky Feline

Homepound: Paris, Texas

Personal Heroes: Paris Hilton and Morris the Cat

Pet Parent: Antoine, top chef

WHAT?
I'M JUST CHILLIN'.

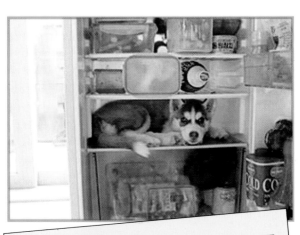

Name: Doobie

Homepound: Venice Beach, California

Career Objective: None

Signature Designer: Billabong

Favorite Thing: Catching husky waves
in between kielbasa breaks in the minibar

Pet Parent: Barbie N., motivational speaker

Erica hops on the subway
to her launch party, while
Fendi takes the town car.

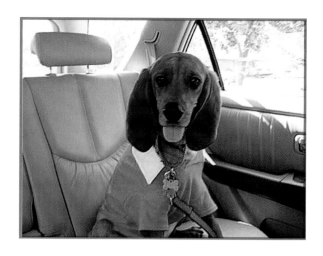

Chmurka moonlights as a document shredder to earn a little extra kibble around the holidays.

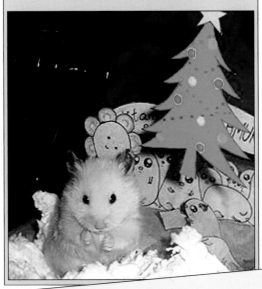

Name: Chmurka

Hometank: Washington, D.C.

Favorite Holiday: Christmas

Special Skill: Running around in balls

Pet Parent: Ben L., congressional page

With Brenda off to school,
Spot catches up on
The Young and the Restless.

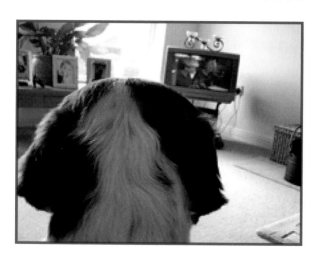

TJ FORMS HIS OWN
BLUE MAN GROUP.

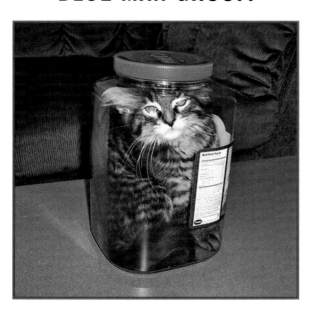

GARDENIA INVESTIGATES THE FUNKY SMELL IN THE CRISPER.

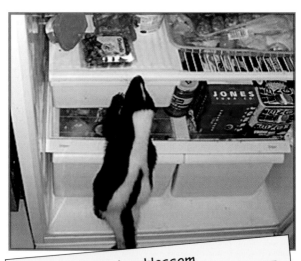

Name: Gardenia Loveblossom
AKA: Stinky Stinkblossom
Homepound: Almost Heaven, West Virginia
Platform: For the world to understand that it's who you are and not how you smell that counts. To get to whatever is in that crisper. And world peace.
Pet Parent: Elizabeth R., pageant title holder

IN THE PAWS OF SOMETHING LARGER THAN THEMSELVES, LOUIE AND OLIVE ELOPE.

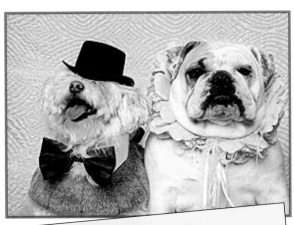

Names: Louie and Olive
Wedding Theme: Putting on the dawg
Theme Song: "Puppy Love"
Gown Designed by: Vera Wag

**VIOLET AND PETUNIA
PRACTICE THEIR SISTER ACT.**

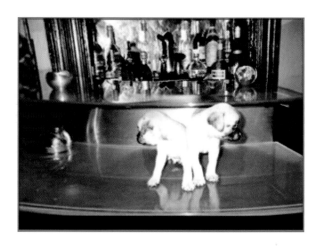

Unbeknownst to Andy,
while he is off servicing other people's
pools, Eddie throws his biweekly
"come pee in my pool" party.

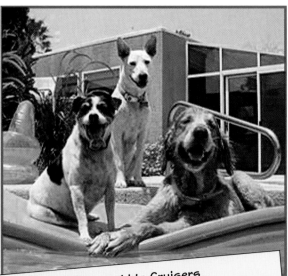

Names: Eddie and his Cruisers

Homepound: Sun City, Arizona

Future Goal: Get a bigger raft

Pet Peeves: Leash laws and "no peeing in the pool" signs

Pet Parent: Andy the Pool Guy

TWO EARS
IN A BUCKET . . .

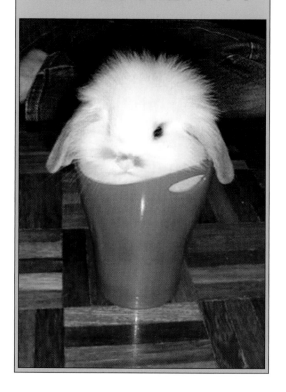

I HATE BIG BUTTS AND I CANNOT LIE.

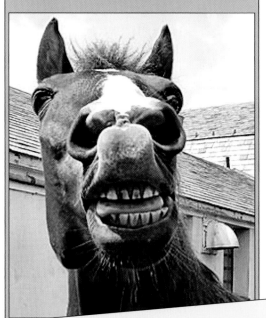

Name: Notorious Hor-Sey
Favorite Music: Rap and hip-hop
Musical Influences: Sir Mix-A-Lot, Elvis
Pet Parent: Earl V., country and western singer

With Kendra off running the dating service, Rapunzel gets ready to kiss yet another frog.

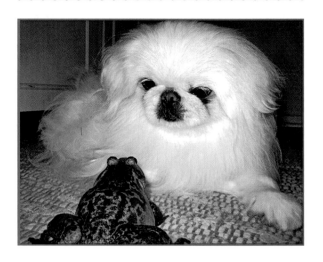

BUD ASSUMES THE POSITION.

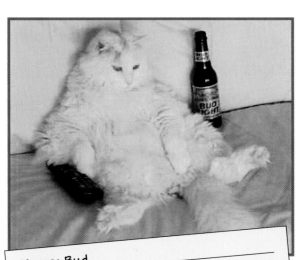

Name: Bud

Homepound: Chi-Town

Favorite Team: Da Bears

Current Occupation: Manager of the remote control, standing in as substitute beer cozy, licking his own butt

Special Skill: Can spit up a hairball on cue

Pet Parent: Cassandra N., chief cook and bottle washer

With the Abernathys gone so much
of the time during planting season,
Lila and Cleo start to drink their lunch
on the rocks.

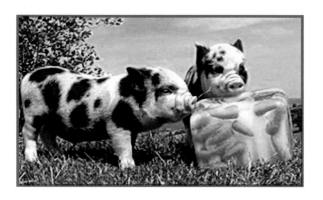

IS IT CHRISTMAS *YET*?

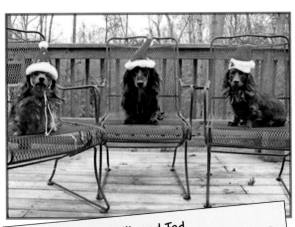

Names: Heidi, Chili, and Ted

AKA: The Three Amigos

Homepound: The cracker and cookie aisle at Wal-Mart

Favorite Things: Crackers and Wal-Mart

Dislikes: Cats and stupid hats

Pet Parent: Tina N., office manager/secret Santa administrator

HELLO? HELLO?
WRONG EXTENSION.

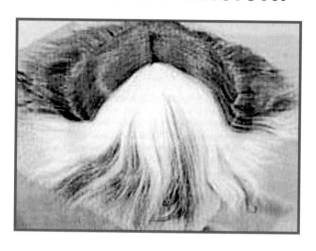

With Mike away working
the kinks out of Windows Vista,
Peaches falls crazy in love with her Mac.

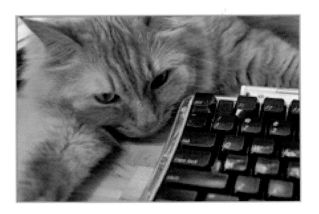

THEO, VINCENT, AND GAUGUIN
ARE STUMPED WHY PETER
HAS TO WORK SO MUCH.

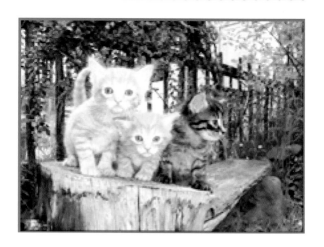

While Brian is feeding the machine, Harmony waits for his lunch.

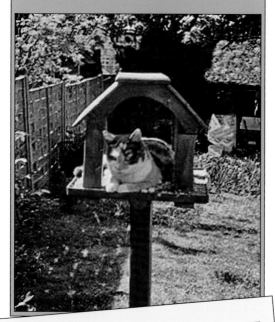

Name: Harmony

Homepound: Where the birds are

Hobbies: Birds, worms, slow-moving mice, and interspecies tolerance

PEEPING TOM
CLAIMS ANOTHER VICTIM.

**While Mike is running City Hall,
Rudy switches to lights.**

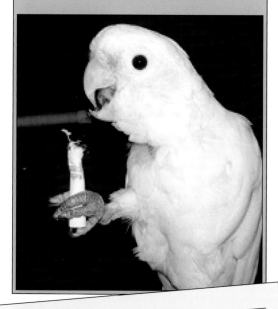

Name: Rudy

Homepound: New York, New York

Pet Peeves: Nonsmoking bars and restaurants

Pet Parent: Mike B., mayor

Peyton learns that it takes a thick skin, and often a hard hat, if you want to get the cheese.

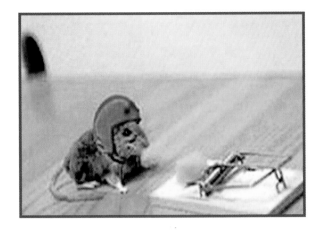

Amanda is answering phones all day, but Gizmo is waiting for tonight!

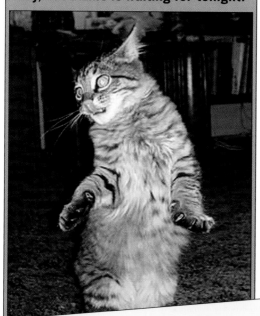

Name: Gizmo

AKA: Kitty From the Block

Career Objective: Backup dancer for J. Lo

Signature Scent: Glow

Pet Parent: Carol R., hotel reservations clerk/wake-up call operator

Inspired by Tony's constant complaining about his workload, Diesel learns to clone himself.

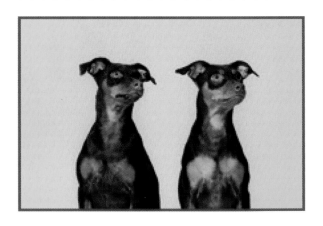

PSST . . .
I THINK THEY LEFT
THE TREAT JAR OPEN.

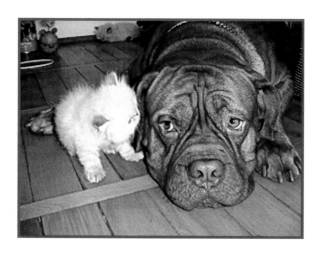

With the Salvos off making hay,
Fluffy and Brandy sneak into the pasture
to express the love that dares not speak
its nei-ei-ei-eighm.

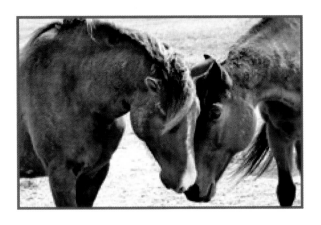

At his Tuesday lunch club,
Roland refuses to eat another bite
until somebody passes
the Grey Poupon.

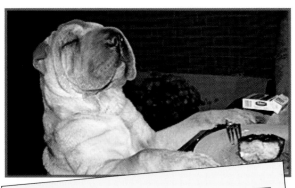

Name: Roland
AKA: The King
Homepound: Easy Street
Favorite things: Filet mignon and Smackos
Pet Peeves: French's, Gulden's
Pet Parent: Frank L., food critic

ROWDY DRIES OUT.

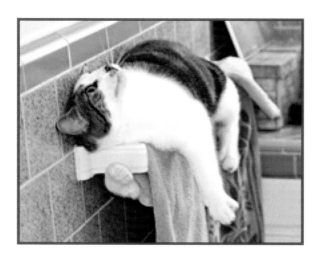

While Beth is away scheduling appointments, Elvis waits for the iceman to cometh.

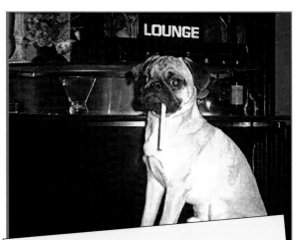

Name: Elvis
Homepound: Any Broadway bar stool
Occupation: Professional dreamer
Pet Peeves: Elvis impersonators and pawdicures
Personal Mantra: I did not inhale
Pet Parent: Eugene O., booking agent

THANK GOD THEY'RE FINALLY GONE!

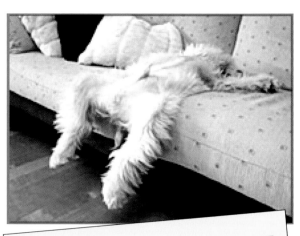

Name: Hopper

Homepound: Oblivion

Career Objective: Dogumentary filmmaker

Current Occupation: Slacker

Pet Parents: Bill and Cindy, career counselors

MRS. DALLOWAY SAYS SHE'LL
BUY THE FLOWERS HERSELF.

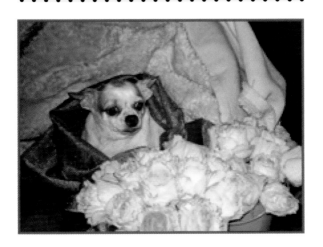

FOR GOD'S SAKE, *PLEASE, SOMEONE,* TAKE ME *OUT!*

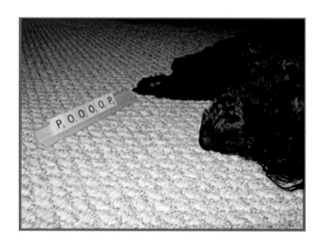

RUFUS AND ALMODOVAR
BUILD THEIR OWN
FOOD CHAIN.

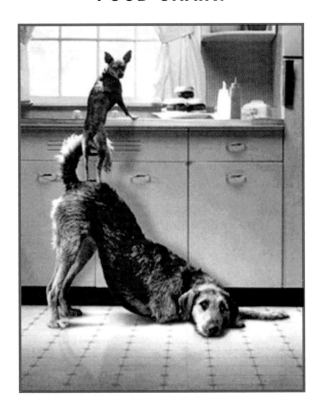

LUCY AND DESI PRACTICE
THE DOG PADDLE.

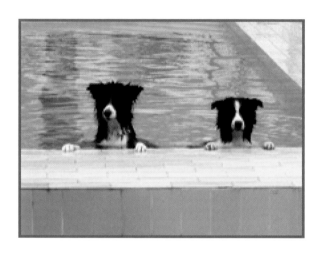

AH, COME ON, REF!

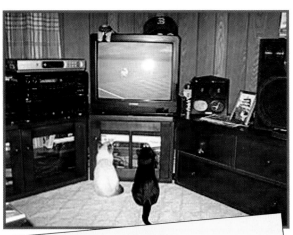

Names: Storm and Logan

Relationship: Brother and sister

Homepound: Beantown

Special Skills: Watching baseball and playing fetch

Pet Parent: Mike M., ref

SIMBA ROLLS OVER.

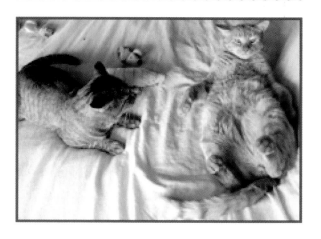

SPIKE CHEATS
ON HIS DIET.

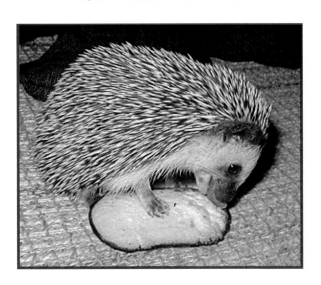

Henry, Harvey, and Hopalong realize
that three doesn't have to be a crowd.

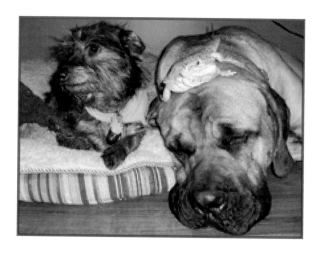

Wicked has been watching too much Nickelodeon again.

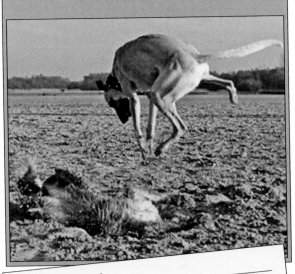

Name: Wicked

Homepound: In the funny papers

Career Objective: Star of his own animated adventure series

Current Occupation: Crazy-ass hound

Favorite TV Shows: *Scooby-Doo* and *Jackass*

Pet Parent: Petra K., animator

Maggie goes back to bed and dreams
of a time when Greenies grow on trees,
dog beds are all 800-thread count,
and her parents work from home.

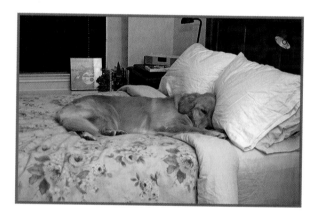

PINTA WANTS YOU
TO WANT HER.

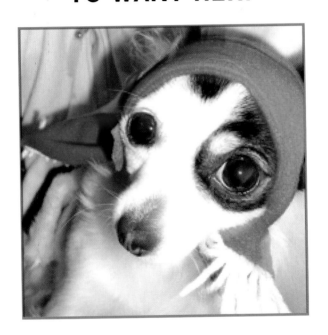

GINGER DOES
HER LEG LIFTS.

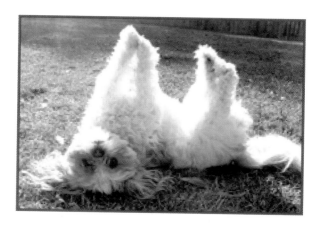

PARIS TRIES TO GET PICKED UP.

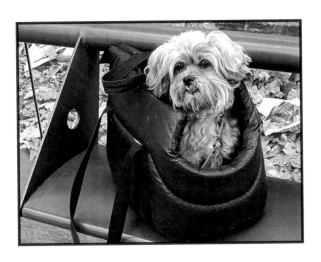

FRANK KNOWS IT
PAYS TO ADVERTISE.

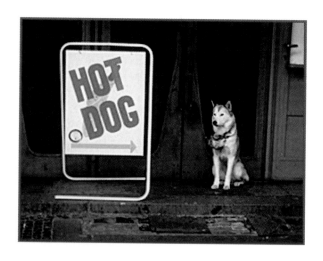

After consuming an entire bag of kibble, Bogart finally gives in to the laws of physics.

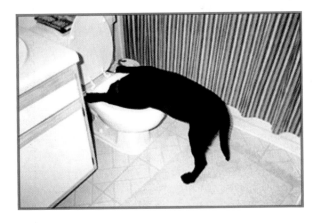

Andy is still working in the towering sky-
scrapers of Manhattan while Starbuck
works through his pile of *New Yorkers*.

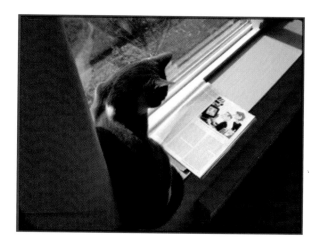

ELVIS, DAISY, BERT, AND BUDDHA KEEP THE CHAIR WARM.

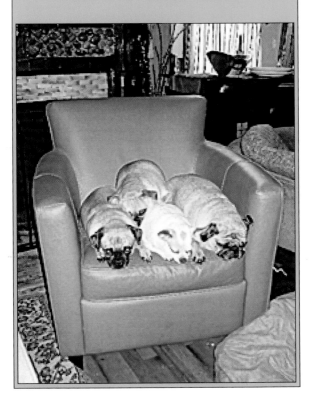

Since Andy's promotion, the Nelsons' future looks so bright that Mister feels compelled to break out the big shades.

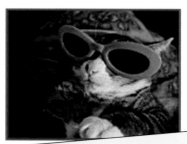

Name: Mister Leonardo da Kitty

AKA: Mister Cool

Pet Peeve: Food bowls that are half empty

Hobbies: Eating, bird-watching, and napping on his polar-bear rug, like this

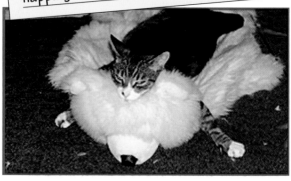

EBONY AND IVORY GRAB A PAW FOR RACIAL UNITY HOLLA!

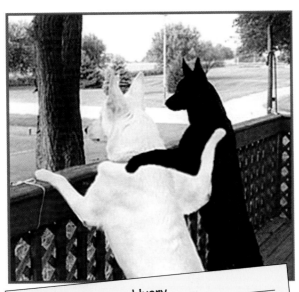

Names: Ebony and Ivory

Relationship: Soul brothers

Homepound: The City of Brotherly Love

Favorite Common Interests: Challenging stereotypes based on color, watching the grass grow

TOMMY TRIES TO EAT
THE *WHOLE* THING.

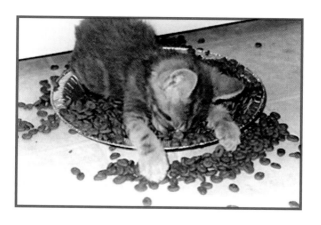

Qin and Pao double their pleasure and double their fun.

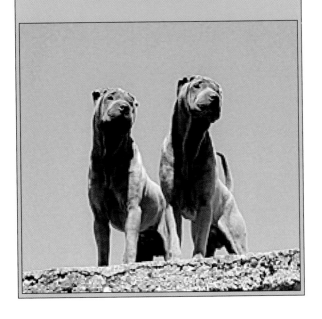

Although Tina's shift ended an hour ago, Toby can't walk away from the table.

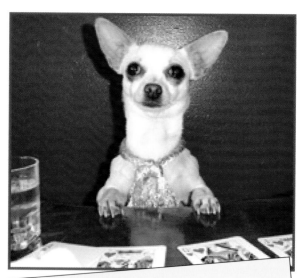

Name: Toby the Tiger
Homepound: Vegas, baby!
Occupation: Card shark and bed hog
Pet Peeves: Cheats and fitted sheets
Personal Mantra: Shut up and deal!
Pet Parent: Tina R., croupier

SYD SEES THE LIGHT.

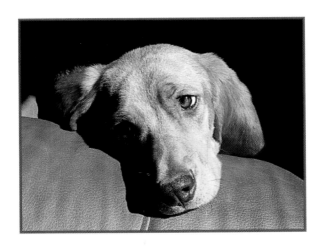

Unbeknownst to Rabbi Goldfarb,
Yentl has a secret.

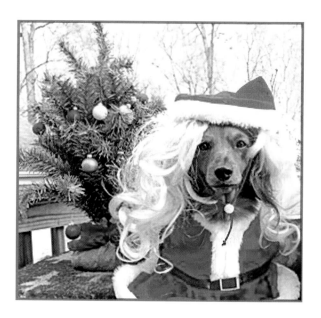

While Ambassador Wilson is off forging treaties, Goliath learns that the biggest dog doesn't always get the bone.

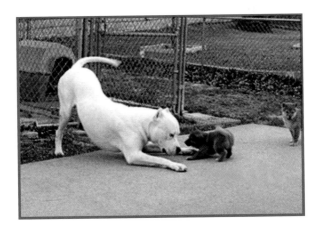

TUTTER GETS POTTED.

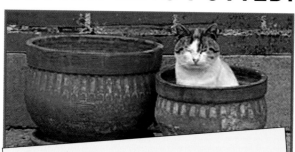

Name: Tutter

Homepound: Aarhus, Denmark

Current Occupation: Barn cat

Biggest Fear: That yellow hose

Fondest Dream: To grow a softer bed from seed

Update: Sometimes dreams come true . . .

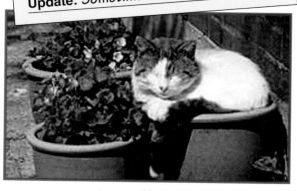

While Gwen is away teaching yoga,
Bandit gives in to a Big Mac attack.

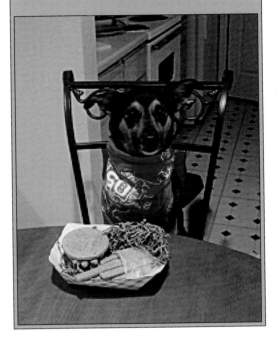

IN A STUNNING REVERSAL,
FLUFFY ATTEMPTS TO KEEP
HIS MOUTH OUT OF THE SHOE.

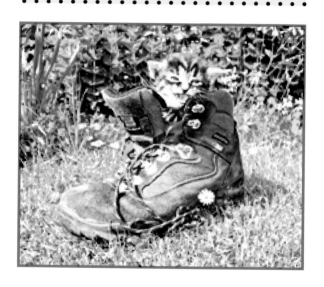

SNOOPY STEWS
IN HIS OWN JUICES.

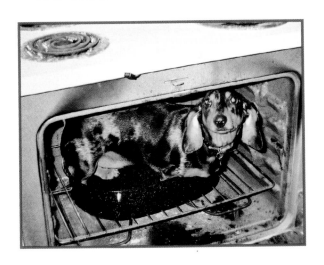

**WANDA THINKS
AULD ACQUAINTANCE SHOULD
BE FORGOT ALREADY!**

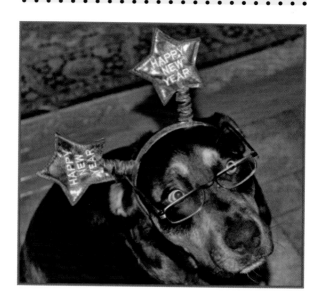

While Brian is at work
throwing his weight around,
Dante is defying gravity.

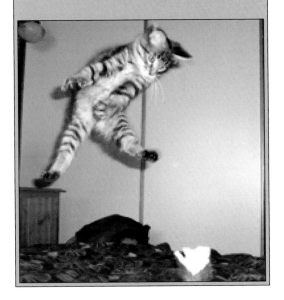

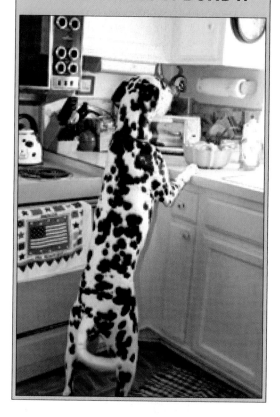

JIGGS BAKES A BUNDT.

With Tina safely away at
a Mary Kay convention, Gigi
and Colette suffer to be beautiful.

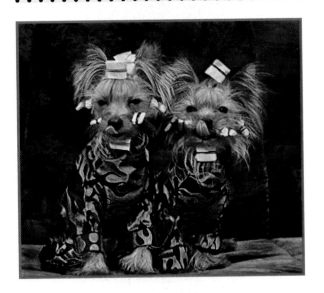

Since Rachel started leaving early
to hit the gym before work,
Sophie frequently finds herself
at the bottom of a huge pot of carbs.

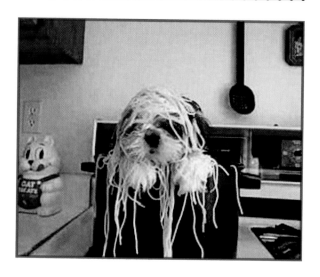

GO AHEAD,
MAKE MY DAY!

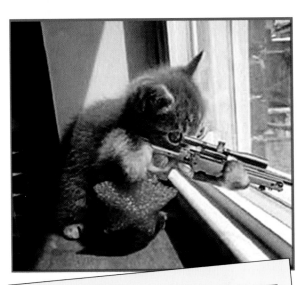

Name: Trigger

Homepound: Hollywood, California

Idol: Charlton Heston

Pet Parent: Hiram W., postal worker

Little do Pookie's parents know
that while they are slaving away
at the DMV, she's out thrill riding.

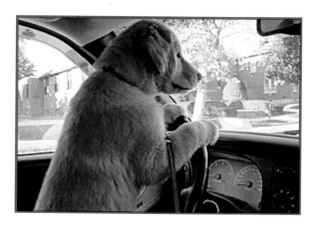

Riley has always depended on the kindness of strangers.

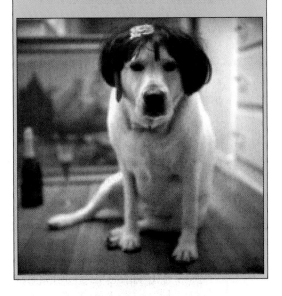

**Bubble tries to get motivated
to do crunches.**

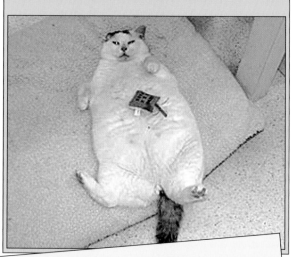

Name: Bubble

AKA: Bubble Butt

Favorite Position: Flat on her back with all four paws in the air

Pet Peeves: Catzines that promote unrealistic body-image expectations, Suzanne Somers, and stairs

Pet Parent: Marisella R., spin class instructor

**MANDY IS LATE FOR THE DENTIST
AND BERT REALIZES HE FORGOT
TO FLOSS.**

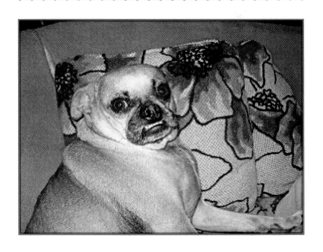

**While Kandy and Bob are meeting
with the florist after work,
Booter eats the seating plans.**

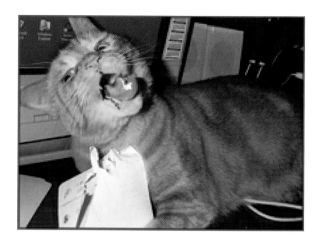

TITO IS GONNA ROCK N' ROLL ALL NIGHT.

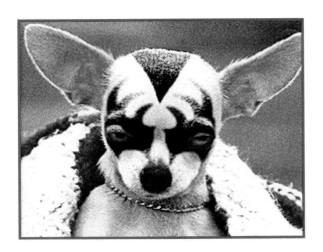

TABBY TAKES
A CAT NAP.

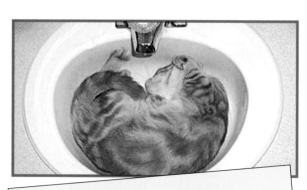

Name: Tabby Cat

AKA: The Tabster

Homepound: Anywhere above plumbing

Pet Peeve: When people want to brush their teeth

Special Skill: Vast knowledge of modern art

**Secretly,
Butch feels most comfortable
in his princess chair.**

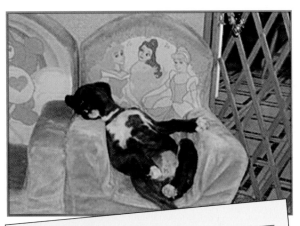

Name: Butch
AKA: Princess Poopsalot
Homepound: Motor City
Occupation: Security guard
Career Goal: Entertainer

Now that Chris is teaching voice full-time, Caruso learns to sing solo.

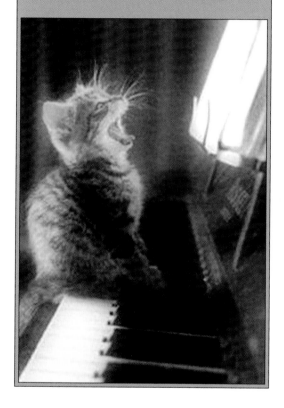

HOPPER
HANGS FOUR.

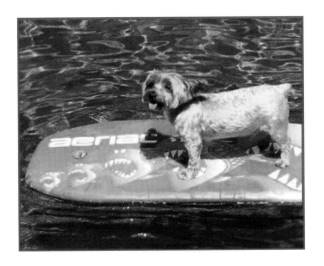

Tiger is only two strokes away from breaking the world record, and the lamp.

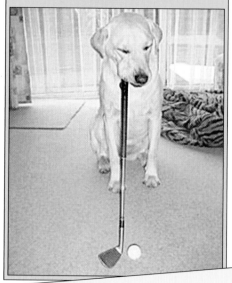

Name: Tiger

Homepound: The nearest putting green

Winning Philosophy: Keep your eye on the ball—and the plate-glass windows

**GOOSE LEFT HIS HEART
IN FENWAY PARK.**

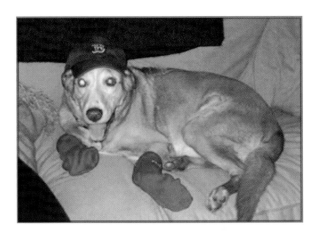

While the Ramirezes
are at the bank, Bentley searches
for change in the couch.

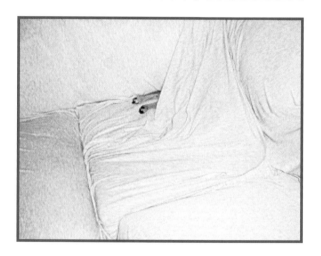

TOBY PLOTS VENGEANCE
ON HER LOOK-ALIKE.

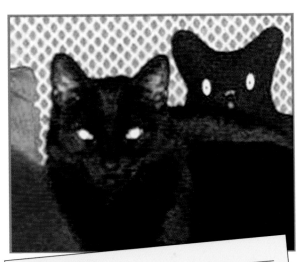

Name: Toby
Homepound: Brooklyn, New York
Favorite Things: Crossing people's paths just to freak them out, sleeping on his mistress's head
Pet Peeve: That Ugly Doll
Pet Parents: Pia and Mina, stand-up comedians

Effie re-creates crucial scenes from *Dreamgirls* on YouTube.

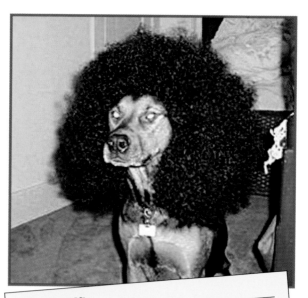

Name: Effie

Homepound: Tin Pan Alley

Favorite Movie: *Dreamgirls*

Personal Mantra: I'm staying, and you, and you, and you—you're gonna love me

When Chad's in court,
Toffee exercises her divine rights.

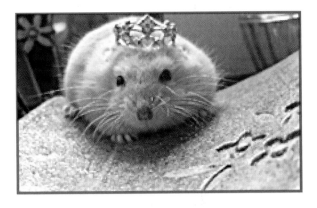

Momo gets caught speeding again (and she's *not* happy!).

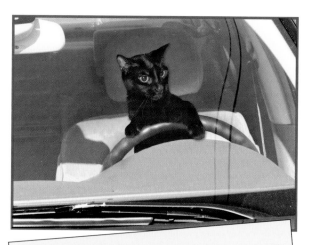

Name: Momo

Homepound: Tupelo, Mississippi

Current Occupation: Fat cat

Favorite Band: Little Feet

Pet Parent: Neil M., state trooper

BEND IT
LIKE BUBBLES.

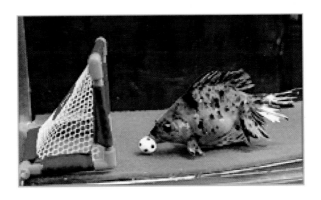

MRS. BEASLEY
GETS LIT.

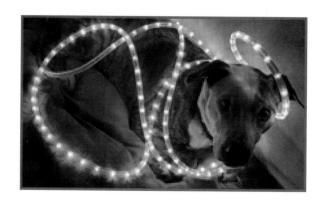

REM SEES
DEAD PEOPLE.

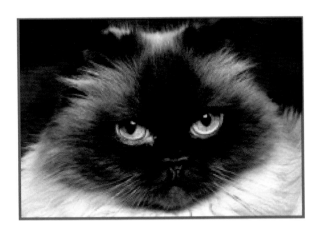

HAIR OF THE DOG.

HeadOn. Apply directly to the forehead.
HeadOn. Apply directly to the forehead.
HeadOn. Apply directly to the forehead.

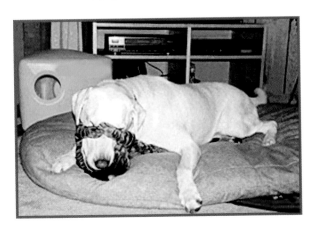

There once was a bird
from Nantucket . . .

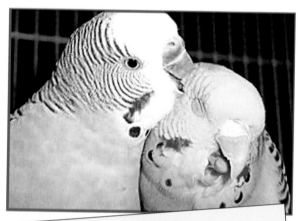

Names: Frankie and Honey

Homeperch: A gilded cage

Favorite Things: Sitting in a tree, K-I-S-S-I-N-G, sharing off-color limericks

Theme Song: "All You Need Is Love"

Pet Parent: Kathy L., sexpert

When Ed gets home from a long, hard day,
Snowflake finds it hard to pull himself away
from his favorite little hole in the wall.

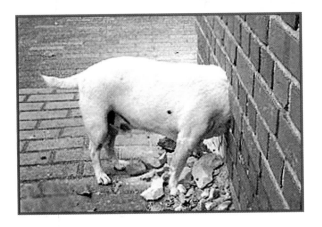

While Madison is at the bakery decorating other people's cakes, Shelby waits patiently to blow out her candles.

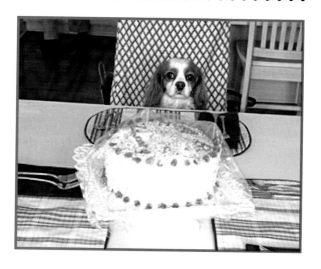

Borris knows the mail carrier always rings twice.

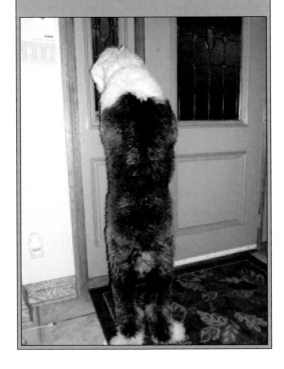

Kisa mentally undresses her toys.

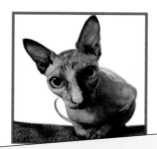

Name: Kisa
AKA: Mistress Kisa, the Sphinx
Turn-ons: Nudity, spanking, pants-ing teddy bears
Turnoffs: All clothing and Hello Kitty
Pet Parent: Vera W., fashion designer

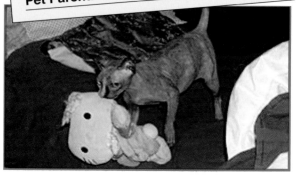

With Alison working long hours polishing everybody else's smiles, Fluffy takes matters into her own paws and attends to her own dental hygiene.

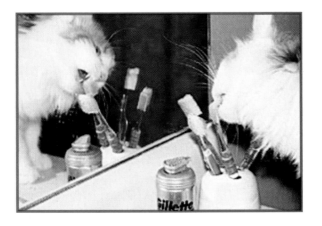

Danielle and Todd are out playing the odds, and Ivory finds his own slot machine.

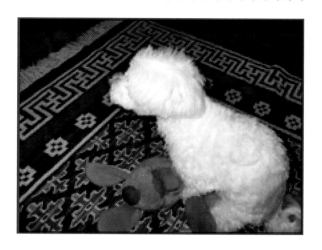

CHUBS WONDERS IF HE'LL FIT OUT THE DOOR TODAY.

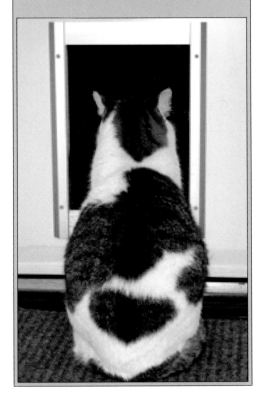

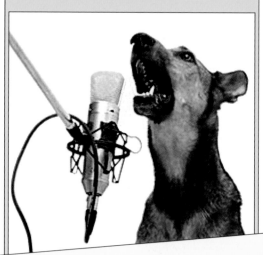

Woody brings his message to the people.

Name: Woody
Homepound: Hometown, USA
Personal Heroes: Woody Guthrie, Bob Dylan, and Lassie
Career Objective: Champion of the working breeds
Personal Mantra: This dog barks at fascists and parked cars

DON'T *PUSH* ME!

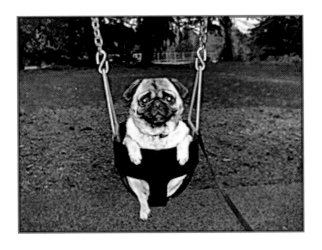

Hal sinks to an all-time low.

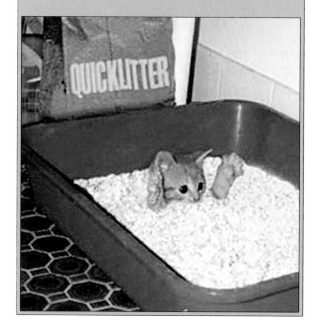

BRUTUS PUTS A NEW PICTURE UP ON HIS CATSTER PAGE.

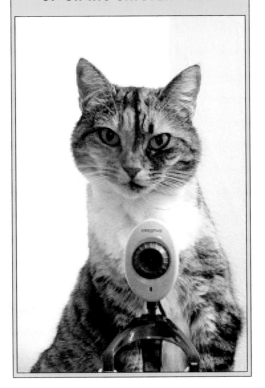

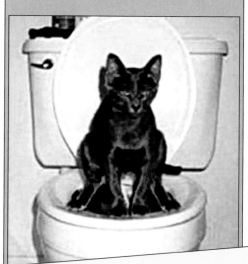

What? It's not rocket science.

Name: Einstein
AKA: Poop Stain
Life Goals: To learn how to flush, and to pioneer technology that can send all dogs to the moon
Pet Peeve: People who close the lid
Personal Heroes: Mr. Whipple, Stephen Hawking, Toonces the Driving Cat
Pet Parent: Steve J., rocket scientist

With Bill working all-you-can-eat night at the Happy Burger, Sushi enjoys her signature dish.

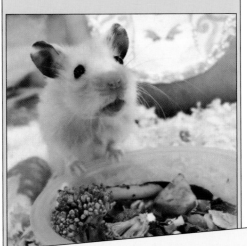

Name: Sushi

Career Objective: Minimalist-inspired interior designer

Current Occupation: Mouse in a house

Pet Peeves: Cats, rococo

Secret Fantasy: To someday own her own bento box

Pet Parent: Philip W., short-order cook

Precious proves once again that what sets her apart from other animals is her ability to accessorize.

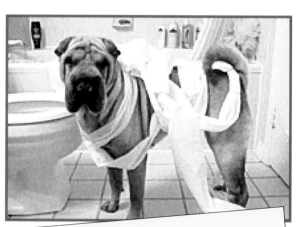

Name: Precious

AKA: Just Precious

Signature Designers: Bark Jacobs, Chewy Vuitton, Mr. Whipple

Personal Mantra: Real sharpeis have wrinkles

Pet Parent: Anita R., Avon lady

**POOKA THINKS WE ARE ALL
SOFA KING WE TODD DID.**

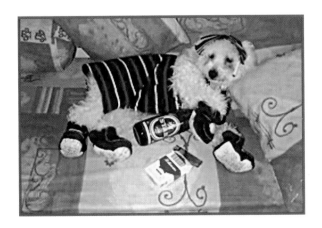

YES, IT'S A MESS, BUT IS IT *ART*?

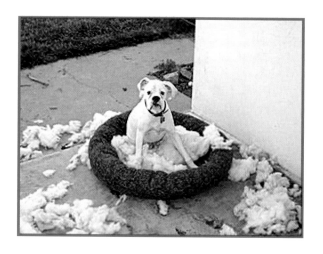

BLAZE FINDS A NEW KONG.

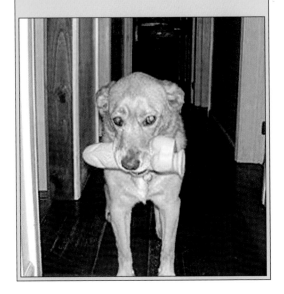

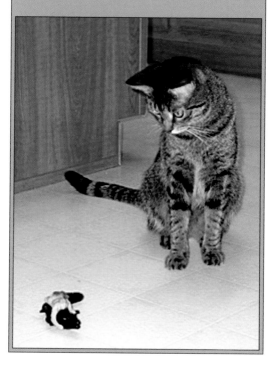

Mittens encounters his first unidentified crawling object as Calvin is off tracking the skies over North America.

While Kathleen's off pushing paper,
Billy dreams of winning
the big game for the Steelers.

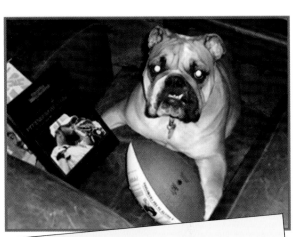

Name: Billy Mumphrey

Homepound: NYC, although he left his heart in Pittsburgh

Personal Heroes: Jerome "The Bus" Bettis, Lady in *Lady and the Tramp*, and Seinfeld

Pet Parent: Kathleen S., marketing consultant

While the Cavenaughs are on I-95 stuck in gridlock, Boris and Rimu take time to smell the lavender.

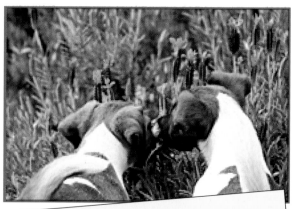

Names: Boris and Rimu

Homepound: Kaiapoi, New Zealand

Favorite Things: High-speed aerial leaps, picking flowers, playing tugga, each other

While Wayne is busy trying to shrink the deficit, Big Mac gets supersized.

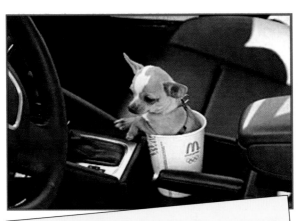

Name: Big Mac
Homepound: The cup carrier
Career Objective: Leader of a taco revolution
Current Occupation: Pocket pooch

Tired of life at the bottom,
Speedy straps on his fin and
practices swimming with the sharks.

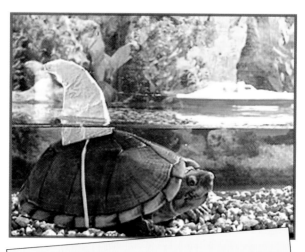

Name: Speedy

AKA: Jaws

Special Skill: Dry wit

Area for Improvement: Cold feet

Pet Parent: Phil C., retail

STEP OFF!

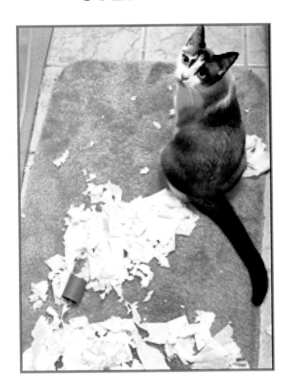

While the Smiths are off running the family shake shack, Nathan and Oscar check out the competition.

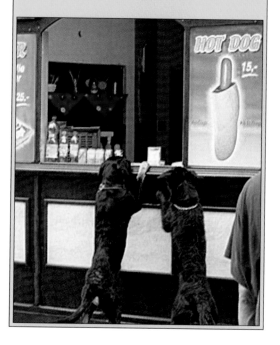

ROTFL.

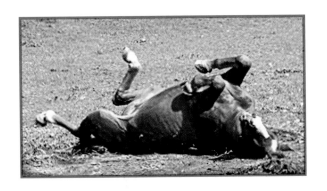

FAT DAISY SPIES
A FRENCH FRY.

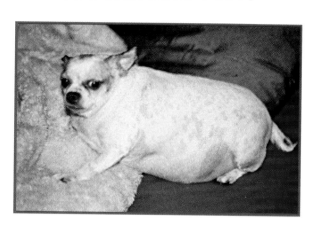

VINNIE REALIZES THAT NICK HAS BEEN COOKING WITH TOO MUCH GARLIC AGAIN.

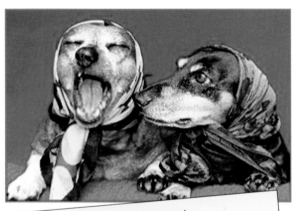

Names: Nicholas and Vincent

Relationship: Babushka brothers

Favorite Movies: Yentl, Sunset Boulevard

Favorite Things: Trying on clothes in Mommy's closet, QVC

Pet Parent: Sylvia R., mystery shopper

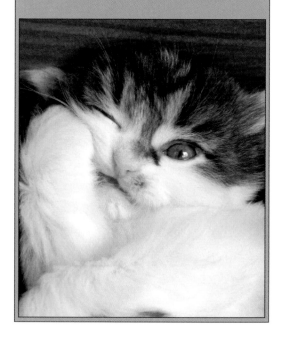

JONNY PONDERS
THE ETERNAL QUESTIONS.

Chewbacca discovers that, girl, one bad apple don't always spoil the whole bunch.

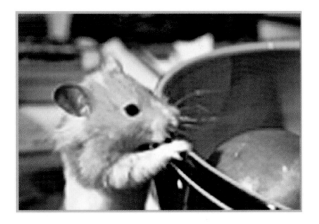

ROZ WAITS PATIENTLY FOR SOMETHING TO MOVE.

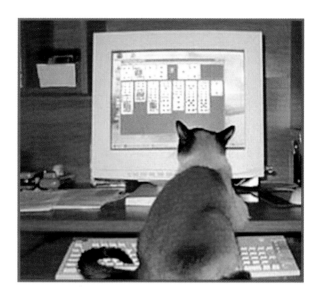

> **While Melvin is off crunching numbers, Alaska sets off in search of the Bridge to Terabithia.**

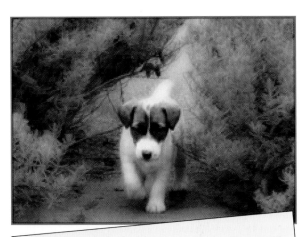

Name: Alaska

Homepound: The lavender fields of New Zealand

Favorite Things: Long walks with the wind in his ears, moonlight

Pet Parent: Melvin S., CPA

**Despite his pop-up wings,
Flat Stanley fails to achieve
the third dimension.**

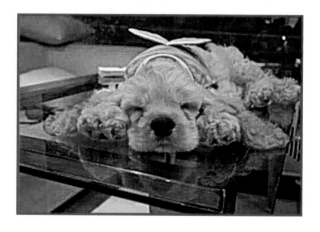

ANYBODY NEED
A LIGHT?

SPIKE MOONLIGHTS
AS ZZ TOP'S MASCOT

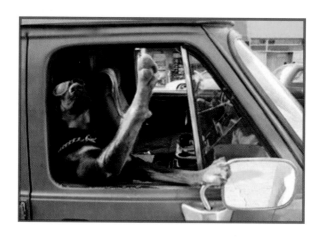

WHO MOVED OUR CHEESE?

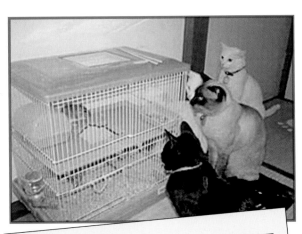

Name: Widget

AKA: Mud

Homepound: In his cage not bothering anybody

Special Skills: Really easy to get along with, really a very nice mouse, not the kind of a mouse that would under any circumstances move anybody else's cheese ever

Career Objective: Living

While Bev and Jason are out publicizing their latest book . . .

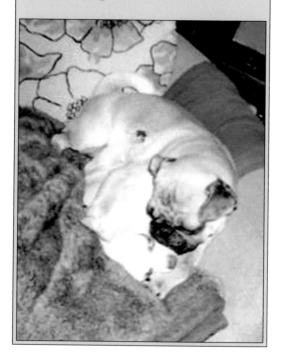

. . . ELVIS AND DAISY BUILD A FAMILY.

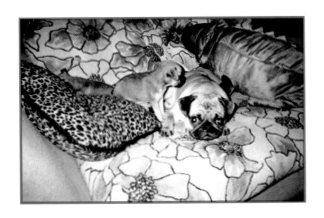

Luke waits patiently for somebody
to get home from work and pass
the potatoes already.

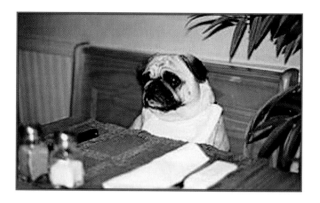

Realizing that they live right next door to an upscale dog biscuiterie, Tosca and Karma reach out to the neighbors.

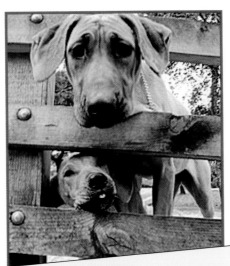

Names: Tosca and Karma

Homepound: Buenos Aires

Career Objectives: Bigger yard, fewer fences

Favorite Things: The tango, "La Bamba," biscuits

Personal Mantra: Don't fence me in

> This would explain the sand
> in the Nelsons' sheets.

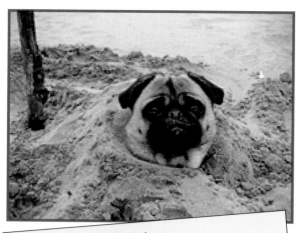

Name: Harry Houdini

Homepound: Hyannispug

Special Skills: Disappearing into thin air, escaping in the nick of time, digging

Heroes: David Blaine, Frank from *Men in Black*

While Lamont is off fixing pipes,
Sable wonders who forgot to flush.

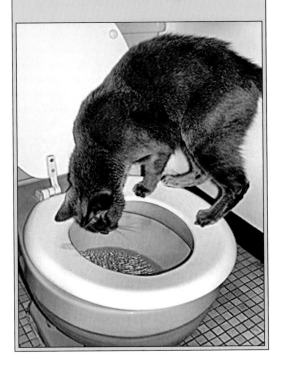

Gated out of the treat zone *again*,
Peanut counts to ten.

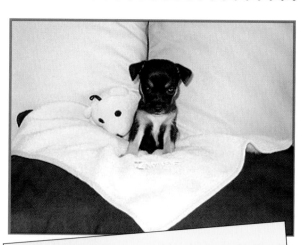

Name: Peanut

AKA: Trouble

Homepound: The doghouse

Special Skills: Irresistible and adorable
as hell, and it's a good thing too

Personal Mantra: Serenity now!

Pet Parent: Lamar T., anger management
counselor

While Stan's off tuning up engines,
Harley doubles down.

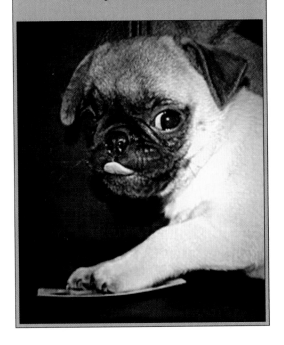

**One small step for Petey,
one giant leap for canine kind.**

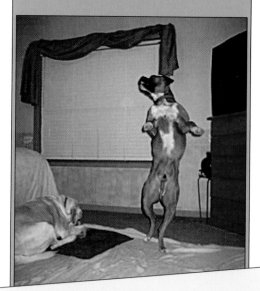

Name: Petey

AKA: The Missing Link

Fondest Dream: Edible dog-food cans

Deepest, Darkest Secret: Wishes he was an only dog

Pet Parent: Irena C., dog walker

BENJI LEARNS TO CHUG-A-PUG.

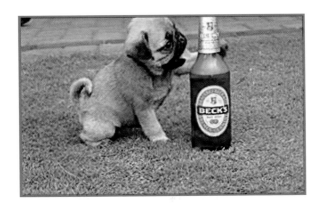

BARBIE OUTGROWS HER DREAMHOUSE.

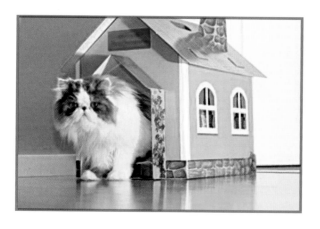

Bored with life under a heat lamp, Shep crawls toward financial freedom.

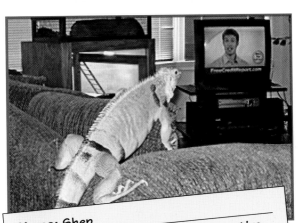

Name: Shep
Career Objective: Advertising executive
Current Occupation: Reptile
Special Skills: Sitting motionless under a hot lamp for hours and pooping in the bathtub
Favorite Pastime: Watching commercials
Pet Parents: Troy and Robert, jingle composers

**CRUISER THINKS GLOBALLY
BUT ACTS LOCALLY.**

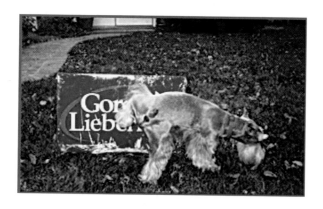

Shhhhhhhh!

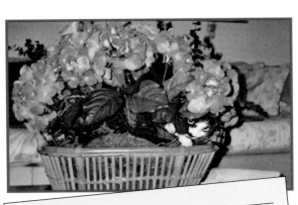

Name: Foxy

Homepound: Location confidential

Current Occupation: Undercover operative

Special Skills: Blending in seamlessly with table arrangements, quick escapes

WHAT MAKES YOU THINK
I WON'T NIP YOU?

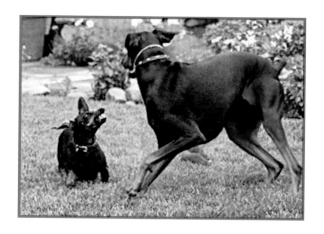

Cuddles and Sparky are *so* glad they're *finally* gone!

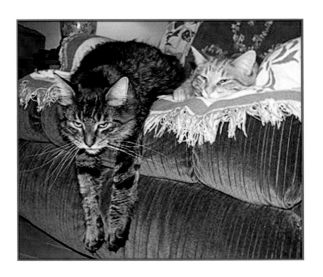

When it's Herman's day to do the dishes, he really throws himself into the job.

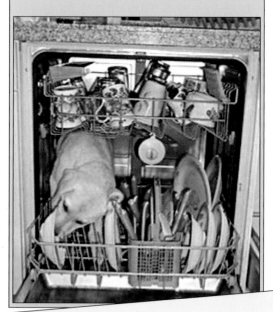

Name: Herman

AKA: Turbo-Tongue, the Pre-rinse Puppy

Favorite Thing: People who don't clean their plates

Pet Peeve: Jet-Dry baskets

Up for performance review,
Kaley bones up on her
fundamentals.

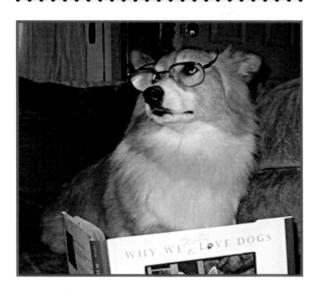

Chloe naps between the horns of her dilemma as Ina helps others with theirs.

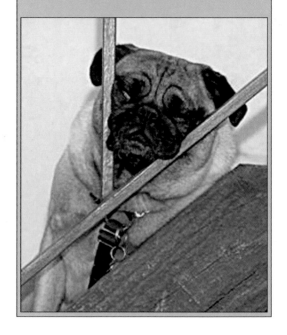

BAINE CULTIVATES NEGATIVE COPING BEHAVIORS.

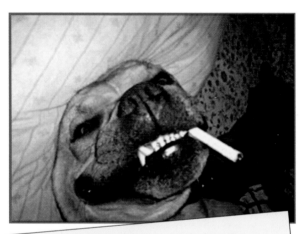

Name: Bad Boy Baine

Homepound: Jerseyside

Occupation: Friend o' mine

Personal Mantra: Fuhgedaboudit

Pet Parent: Joe Bag a' Donuts, waste management

ONCE FLUFFY GETS CAUGHT IN A PUPPY-PORN CYCLE, HE CAN BE THERE FOR DAYS.

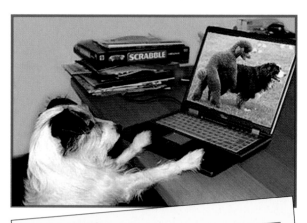

Name: Fluffy

AKA: Fluffy Dot Com

Homepound: Dogster

Looking For: Puppy play and dog-on-dog action

Pet Parent: Lester N., televangelist

Marlin is convinced that one of these days he really will find Nemo.

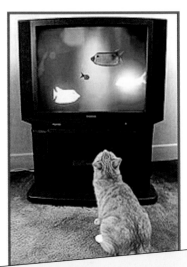

Name: Marlin Brando

Homepound: Omapaw

Career Objective: Gotta get the fish. Gotta get the fish. Gotta get the fish. Get the fish!

Current Occupation: Get the fish. Gotta get the fish. Wait . . . I think I . . . Nope . . . Gotta get the fish. Get the fish!

Pet Parent: Seth B., hypnotist

LITTLE CAT,
BIG DREAMS.

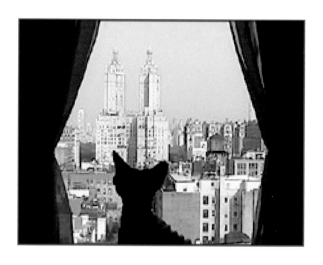

SOPHIE ACHIEVES
NIRVANA.

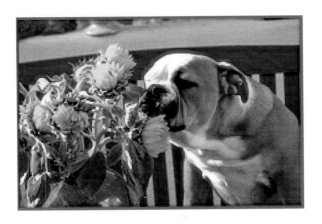

WHILE KERRIE SELLS HOT READS TO BOOKSTORES, RUBY INDULGES IN A PAWDICURE AND DREAMS OF NINE-INCH NAILS

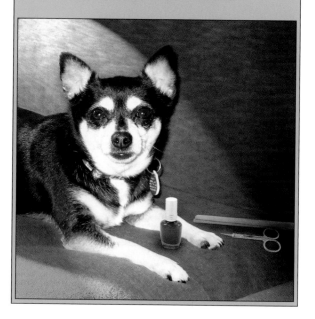

While Erich is off designing bestsellers,
Daisy May discovers that every rose
has its thorn.

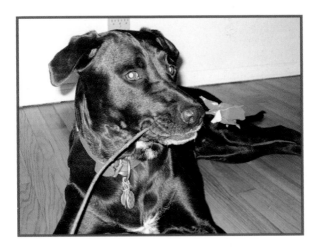

POISON
IS RIDIN' DIRTY.

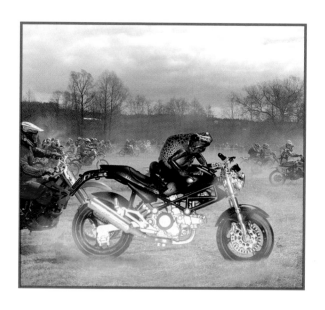

Fed up with the constant taunts
about his plushie,
Butterscotch strikes back.

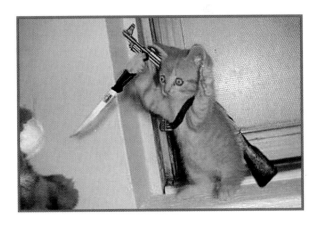

MAX LEAPS
TALL FLIP-FLOPS
IN A SINGLE BOUND.

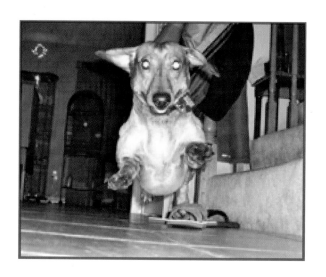

Minnie goes undercover.

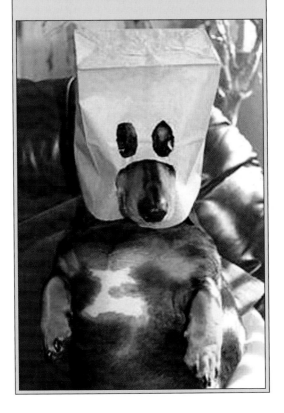

LUCKY AND LUCY
TAKE THE LEAP.

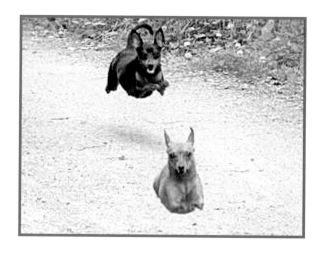

While Elizabeth is off making people famous, Mocha knows who the real star is.

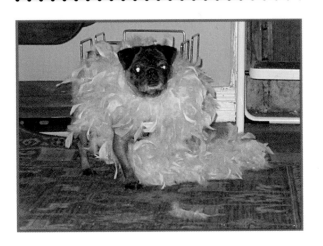

Unbeknownst to Daddy, while he's off opening the bar early, Boss and Topper achieve simultaneous snoregasms.

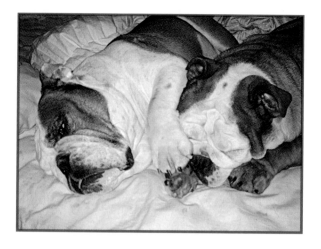

PEPITO LEARNS
WHY LOVE HURTS.

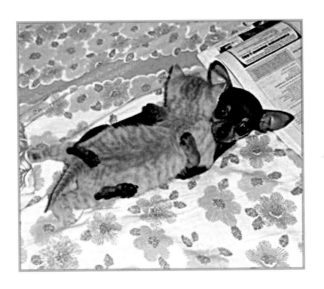

Photo Credits

Beverly West (coauthor of the bestselling *Cinematherapy* series) and Jason Bergund are freelance writers and newlyweds living in pet-obsessed bliss on the Upper West Side of Manhattan with their four dogs, Elvis, Daisy, Buddha, and Bert; their cat, Hamlet; and two turtles. Together, Bev and Jason are the coauthors of *PugTherapy: Finding Happiness, One Pug at a Time*; *Fat Daisy: Inner Beauty Secrets from a Real Dog*; and *TVtherapy: The Television Guide to Life*.